How a Recession Affects You

Jason Porterfield

ROSEN
PUBLISHING®

New York

Published in 2013 by The Rosen Publishing Group, Inc.
29 East 21st Street, New York, NY 10010

Copyright © 2013 by The Rosen Publishing Group, Inc.

First Edition

Library of Congress Cataloging-in-Publication Data

Porterfield, Jason.
How a recession affects you/Jason Porterfield.—1st ed.
      p. cm.—(Your economic future)
Includes bibliographical references and index.
ISBN 978-1-4488-8345-5 (library binding)
1. Recessions. 2. Recessions—United States. 3. United States—
Economic conditions—21st century. I. Title.
HB3716.P673 2013
330.973—dc23

                                                             2012018784

Manufactured in the United States of America

CPSIA Compliance Information: Batch #W13YA: For further information, contact Rosen Publishing, New York, New York, at 1-800-237-9932.

Contents

A family protests eviction from their home. Despite government efforts to help struggling homeowners, the Great Recession brought a wave of foreclosures.

Introduction

For many Americans, the Christmas season of 2008 was a bleak occasion. People shopped for gifts and decorated for the holiday as usual, but the economic situation could not be completely forgotten. An economic crisis earlier in the autumn had knocked the American economy into freefall. In November 2008, the economy had shed 533,000 jobs, the largest monthly loss in decades. By the end of the year, the total number of lost jobs would be more than two-and-a-half million.

Even as family members gathered around Christmas trees and dinner tables to bask in the warm holiday glow, they could not completely avoid feeling the personal impact of the economic situation. Some family members told stories about losing their jobs or taking pay cuts. They confided about how business at their workplaces had slowed, and they were worried about the possibility of being laid off. College seniors graduating in the spring were concerned about job prospects in their field. Everybody had heard about the low sales for the Christmas shopping season, which was reflected in the smaller pile of presents under the tree.

Many Americans were angry, too, at Wall Street, big banks, and the government. The uncertain state of the economy was the result of a financial crisis. In the view of many people, financial institutions had wrecked the economy, only to be bailed out by the government—leaving ordinary Americans suffering financially. People were generally pessimistic, believing that the worst had not yet arrived. Unfortunately, they were correct. Job losses and economic decline continued into 2009. Worse, people began to lose their homes due to bank foreclosures.

The economy is constantly cycling between periods of economic growth and contraction. A recession is a prolonged period—six months or more—of economic contraction. Recessions always bring hard economic times, but the recession that lasted from 2007 to 2009 was bad enough to earn the title of the "Great Recession." Statistics concerning levels of unemployment, bankruptcies, and foreclosures broke records held for decades. About 8.8 million jobs were lost. Even if hiring had rebounded strongly after the recession ended, it would have taken years to bring unemployment back down to prerecession levels. In reality, job creation remained weak long after the end of the recession, leading to long-term unemployment for many Americans.

The recession officially ended in June 2009. At that time, economic expansion began once again, marking the beginning of the recovery. Since then, economists and ordinary Americans alike have watched closely for indications of healthy economic growth. Gradually, many of the sectors of the economy that had collapsed so dramatically in 2008 began to revive. Manufacturing, including the auto industry, saw improvement. Financial markets rebounded, and corporate profits increased. Consumers began spending more freely. Conditions of the housing market remained dire, though some regions saw a slight uptick in sales. Americans, after learning hard financial lessons during the recession, began to allow themselves a little hope for a brighter economic future ahead.

Chapter 1

Roots of the Recession

If you're like most people, you probably wouldn't notice the beginning of a recession. You might observe that houses in your neighborhood are taking longer to sell and wonder if it could indicate an economic slowdown. Your mother or father might mention lower profits or pay cuts and layoffs at work. Most of the time, though, such changes just reflect the normal ups and downs of business. The official starting date of a recession is not announced until many months after the fact, when the National Bureau of Economic Research (NBER) has had time to analyze the relevant economic data.

In December 2007, few people would have guessed that the global economy was on the verge of sliding into a deep recession. In some respects, the economy in the United States appeared to still be growing through the middle of 2008. However, late summer 2007 represented the beginning of one of the deepest and longest recessions in the nation's history. A year later, after the collapse of several major financial firms and a dramatic stock market crash that had set off rounds of layoffs and thrown millions of people out of work, economists were able to put the pieces together and mark the precise point at which the recession started.

The Business Cycle

A recession is generally defined as six months or more of declining gross domestic product (GDP). GDP is the measure of the value of all goods and services that a nation produces. In identifying the turning points of a recession, the NBER examines a number of other important economic indicators in addition to GDP, like income, unemployment levels, industrial production, and sales. Along with a handful of other indicators, these statistics convey a clear idea of the direction in which the economy is heading.

Recessions are a normal part of the business cycle, which is a pattern of alternating economic growth and contraction. The business cycle has four phases: peak, recession, trough, and expansion. The peak is the point at which growth is the highest. After the peak, the economy contracts, resulting in a recession. The trough is the lowest point in the downturn. It is followed by a recovery characterized by expansion and renewed growth.

There have been twelve recessions since the end of the Great Depression, which lasted from 1929 to 1934. Until the Great Recession, the average length of an economic downturn was eleven months. A brief recession that began in 1980 lasted just six months. The longest was the recession that began in 1973 and lasted sixteen months. By contrast,

A protester brandishes a flyer calling on the U.S. Congress and big corporations to take action to put the fourteen million unemployed Americans back to work.

the longest period of economic growth was the nearly ten-year stretch from 1991 to 2001.

The precise beginning of the Great Recession was somewhat difficult to pin down. When defining the start of a recession, the NBER looks for a decline in overall economic activity spread out over several months. In 2008, however, GDP continued to rise through the first half of the year. Stock market numbers and the job market also remained relatively stable. In looking at what had happened to spur the economic downturn that had become obvious by mid-2008, the bureau found that company payrolls had peaked in December 2007 and declined in every month since. During this same period, the real GDP also had fallen. In September 2010, the NBER announced that the recession's trough occurred in June 2009. The economy had started to recover at that point, though the recovery stuttered and stalled several times in the years that followed.

Going Bust

Ultimately, the cause of the Great Recession could be traced to the collapse of the housing market, which had long brought growth to financial institutions and other industries related to homebuilding and real estate. Much of the first decade of the twenty-first century was marked by a housing boom. The price and value of homes increased, and many homes were selling quickly and at a good price. People upgraded to larger houses, and many Americans were able to own a home for the first time. Banks introduced new loan programs that made it easier for people to buy homes. People did not always have to prove that they had a steady income before they were approved for loans. When the housing bubble burst, it set off a credit crisis that shook the global economy. The worldwide recession that resulted was the worst economic downturn since the Great Depression.

During late 2008 and early 2009, hundreds of thousands of jobs were lost each month. Unemployment rose to levels not seen in decades. Home foreclosures increased rapidly, as homeowners were unable to pay their monthly mortgages and banks repossessed their homes.

Few economists predicted that the recession would be so deep or last for so long. Through the spring and summer of 2008, there were worrisome signs of a deepening credit crisis. Banks became unwilling or unable to lend money. In March 2008, the bank JPMorgan Chase acquired Bear Stearns, which was the

A foreclosed home is put on the market. Widespread foreclosures cause overall property values to drop, which in turn leads to more foreclosures.

fifth-largest investment bank on Wall Street. Bear Stearns had been on the brink of collapse after other banks had stopped lending it money due to its deep losses from subprime mortgages that had been defaulted on. The U.S. government supported Chase's acquisition of Bear Stearns, signaling its willingness to reach out and rescue firms if their collapse threatened to have a negative impact on the economy.

The financial industry reached a crisis point later in 2008. On September 8, the government took over Fannie Mae and Freddie Mac, the country's two biggest mortgage lenders. A week after the takeover, the Wall Street investment bank Lehman Brothers went bankrupt. Lehman

Stock values fluctuated wildly during the autumn of 2008 as the market reacted to a credit crisis and looming recession resulting from the bursting of the housing bubble.

Brothers had been one of Wall Street's biggest investment banks, but the U.S. government declined to intervene and rescue the firm.

The news that Lehman Brothers had been allowed to fail shocked the financial industry. The sense of insecurity increased for other troubled financial institutions. On September 16, the government bailed out insurance giant AIG, which had suffered substantial losses insuring risky investments. During the last week of September, the troubled bank Wachovia entered into negotiations to be taken over by Wells Fargo. Another major bank—Washington Mutual—collapsed, declared bankruptcy, and was sold by the government to Chase.

The stock market soon reflected the meltdown in the financial sector. In early October 2008, the Dow Jones Industrial Average experienced its worst losses in history, losing 22 percent of its value over the course of eight days. The losses were a stark contrast to the Dow's performance a year before, when it hit a record high of 14,164 in October 2007. From that peak, the Dow Jones plummeted due to economic uncertainty. Between October 1 and October 10, the Dow dropped from 10,831 to 8,451.

Wall Street and Main Street

The credit crunch worsened as the financial crisis grew deeper. Banks had cut back on lending to each other as investments based on subprime mortgages collapsed. They also slowed their lending to individuals and businesses, and it became more expensive to get a loan. Businesses could not get loans for new investments, while individuals could

Bursting Bubbles

Recessions are often the result of economic bubbles deflating. An economic bubble, or asset bubble, occurs when high demand for an asset causes prices to surge to unsustainable levels. When the market for the asset collapses, the value of the asset crashes. People who invested in the asset lose much of their money if they sell after the bubble bursts and prices collapse. Overall, a popped asset bubble means that a huge amount of wealth has very quickly disappeared from the economy. This significantly impacts financial markets and ripples across other sectors of the economy.

Examples of assets that can create economic bubbles include real estate, stocks, and commodities. One of the catalysts of the Great Depression was the 1929 stock market crash, which followed an economic boom that had taken stocks to record-high prices. A more recent episode was the dot-com bubble of the late twentieth century. Investors flocked to put money into new Internet-based companies, convinced that technological innovation would compensate for a lack of concrete, profit-motivated business plans. By 2001, many promising Internet-based businesses had failed, and technology stocks began to slide, which contributed to a mild recession.

not borrow money for major purchases, such as houses or cars. This had a chilling effect on the economy's health. Even though many banks and financial institutions received bailout money from the government during the fall of 2008, lending did not drastically increase.

In late September 2008, Congress began debating ways to confront the crisis through legislation. The government's top priority was to reestablish confidence in the financial markets, but that marked only the beginning of the government's efforts to restore the nation's economic health. Other industries, such as the auto industry, were in need of government assistance in order to stay afloat. There were also the millions of victims afflicted by the recession, including homeowners in danger of losing their houses and unemployed workers who had lost their jobs.

From the beginning, the government's response to the crisis would prove controversial. The Federal Reserve, chaired by Ben Bernanke, and the U.S. Treasury Department, led by Henry Paulson, had handled the troubled financial institutions on a case-by-case basis, increasing economic uncertainty. On September 18, 2008, Paulson unveiled the $700 billion proposal for the Troubled Asset Relief Program (TARP). According to the plan, the government would buy troubled assets, such as bad mortgages from struggling banks. This would head off bank collapses and help end the credit crunch.

The public and many lawmakers disapproved of the plan. Some opponents protested that it went against the idea of a free market. If a financial institution needed government aid, that indicated it was not strong enough to compete against other institutions. Others felt that the bailouts were wrong on moral grounds because the banks had brought their troubles on themselves with risky business deals. In using public money to rescue them from the

Henry Paulson, secretary of the Treasury, and Ben Bernanke, chairman of the Federal Reserve, testify before Congress on measures taken to stabilize financial markets.

crisis, the government would set a dangerous precedent by rewarding the financial institutions for their irresponsible behavior, rather than punishing them.

Supporters of TARP defended the plan by saying that some financial institutions had become "too big to fail." They argued that if such institutions were allowed to collapse, the entire financial industry would be destabilized. The danger to the national economy outweighed any moral considerations or philosophical disagreements.

After some changes, Congress eventually passed TARP, and the first round of bailouts began in October 2008. Financial institutions received TARP funds, and the government bought up investments based on bad mortgages. By taking bailout money, banks and other financial institutions had to agree to government oversight measures, such as limits on executive pay.

Chapter 2

A Global and National Economic Crisis

During a recession, you might see a family member lose a job. You might find that at school, the size of your class is larger because of budget cuts. A friend might mention that her family has started using food stamps to buy food. You might notice signs on houses saying that the mortgage has been foreclosed.

As effects of the recession begin to influence your everyday life, you might ask, "Why doesn't the government do something?" You wouldn't be the only one calling for government action. During a recession, businesses want tax breaks and banks want government loans. States and local governments want money from the federal government. Unemployed Americans want jobs, and investors want the stock market to rise. Above all, everybody wants an end to the recession and economic insecurity. In crafting and passing a legislative response to a recession, lawmakers must weigh which measures are most likely to bring about an economic recovery.

A California woman fills out an application for food stamps after her family was evicted from their rental home and forced to move into a single motel room.

International Interventions

An economic downturn can affect a single country, a region, or the entire world. The Great Depression, for example, affected the global economy and sent many nations into political turmoil. Countries saw their industrial production fall, which led to high unemployment and lower wages. Banks failed, values of stock markets fell worldwide, and people lost their savings and homes. Governments tried to support their domestic economies by raising tariffs (taxes on imported goods). This worsened the crisis by stifling international trade. Across the globe, countries enacted stimulus measures to revive their economies. In the United States, the ambitious stimulus plan was called the New Deal.

After the Great Depression ended, world leaders established a new international monetary system intended to prevent another such economic disaster. Many nations also enacted new regulations and set up programs that would act as economic safety nets during hard times. In the United States, for example, the Federal Deposit Insurance Corporation (FDIC) was established to ensure that people would not lose their money if a bank failed. Social Security was established to provide for the elderly and disabled.

Today, the world is more economically interconnected than ever before. Trade and investment across national borders have increased. Technology allows for instant communication and financial transactions. When evaluating future economic prospects, American investors and economists look at economic indicators abroad as well as at home. They pay attention to trends such as the bond market in Europe, the stock market in Asia, and the inflation rate in China. Any significant changes can affect the outlook for the American economy. Disasters, such as the 2011 tsunami in Japan, can also have a substantial economic impact.

Because of this economic interdependence, it is now more likely that an economic downturn will spread beyond national borders. Not all recessions spread. Sometimes an economic crisis and its consequences are limited to a particular country or region. In Japan, for example, an economic crisis in the late 1980s led to a "lost decade" of economic stagnation during the 1990s. No other countries were substantially affected.

In 2008, however, the effects of the American financial crisis were immediately felt throughout the global economy. Financial institutions across the world had invested in American mortgage-backed securities that lost value when the housing bubble burst. As the global recession took hold, nations saw the underlying weaknesses in their economies revealed, especially in Europe. Some countries had seen their own housing boom and bust. Stock market

High school students protest austerity measures in Greece. The nation's economic crisis created high levels of unemployment and a lack of teachers and books in schools.

values plunged. Just as in the United States, governments had to bail out investment banks affected by the crisis. A few countries had to apply for emergency aid from the International Monetary Fund (IMF).

Central banks worldwide quickly took action by lowering interest rates, a move that injects money into the economy. Their actions averted a global financial meltdown but did not reverse the deepening recession. During late 2008 through 2009, many nations enacted stimulus packages to revive their economies. China passed a $585 billion stimulus plan, even though the country never officially entered a recession. Japan, Germany, France, Britain, and Italy enacted substantial stimulus measures, along with many other nations of the world.

Government Response

The first actions to stabilize the American economy came from the Federal Reserve, the central bank of the United States. The Federal Reserve, along with the Department of the Treasury, engineered the bank bailouts in late 2008. It also cut interest rates and resorted to nontraditional means of injecting money into the economy.

Over the course of the recession and slow recovery, the Federal Reserve's balance sheet grew from less than $1 trillion to nearly $3 trillion in 2012, meaning that it had pumped over $2 trillion into the economy. These monetary measures included programs that propped up banks, encouraged lending, and supported the mortgage and housing market. Even as the Fed worked to bail out banks and stabilize the economy in late 2008, the Fed

The Recession Up North

Like much of the world, Canada endured a recession that began in 2008. Its economy is closely tied to the United States because of the North American Free Trade Agreement (NAFTA). Americans buy 75 percent of Canadian exports. During the recession, Canada's GDP declined, unemployment levels rose, and exports fell. The Canadian government implemented a $30 billion stimulus plan that included tax breaks, housing construction, infrastructure projects, and relief spending.

But Canada's recession was relatively mild and brief. It ended in June 2009. According to experts, stimulus spending succeeded in promoting economic growth. Consumer spending remained relatively stable throughout the downturn. Although the housing market had declined, values soon returned to prerecession levels.

Part of Canada's relative good fortune lay in the strength of its banking system. In 2008, the World Economic Forum rated Canada's banking system the soundest in the world. Canada's banks are regulated through strict government oversight. They did not take on as much debt as American or European banks. Canadian banks did not loosen lending requirements. During the financial crisis, banks across the world teetered and required government assistance. Canada's banks remained solid and sound.

chairman urged legislators to enact a stimulus plan to energize the economy.

A stimulus plan is a fiscal measure intended to encourage economic activity during a downturn. Fiscal policy, which involves the nation's budget and its spending, is determined by Congress and the president. The principle behind fiscal stimulus is that, during a recession, the economy slows because businesses and consumers are not spending money. A stimulus plan aims to compensate for this lack of spending.

So how does the government achieve this goal? Does it write out a check to every American? In early 2008, when indicators pointed to an economic slowdown, the government did exactly that. The main feature of the $150 billion American Stimulus Act of 2008 was a tax rebate deposited directly into taxpayers' bank accounts or mailed as a check. The bill also included measures intended to encourage investment. Overall, the act failed to forestall the recession.

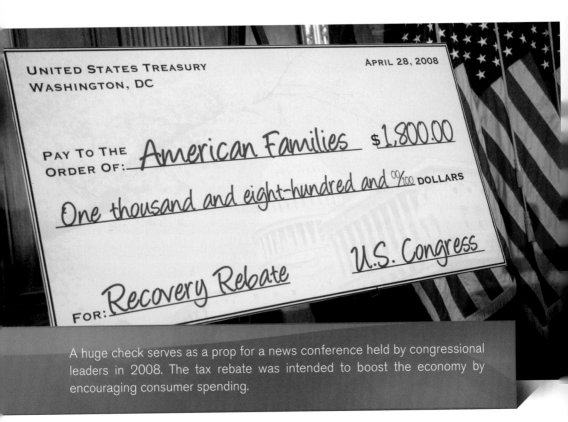

A huge check serves as a prop for a news conference held by congressional leaders in 2008. The tax rebate was intended to boost the economy by encouraging consumer spending.

In 2009, newly inaugurated President Barack Obama made the passage of a stimulus plan his first priority. He laid out his broad priorities and left it to members of the House and Senate to draft the bill. The House and Senate passed two separate measures that were reconciled into the final bill. Although both Republicans and Democrats supported the concept of a stimulus plan, voting was highly partisan. Only three Republican senators voted for the bill. No Republican members of the House voted for the bill. They thought that it was too expensive, even though some economists recommended an even more aggressive stimulus plan. President Obama signed the bill into law in February 2009.

As is typical with stimulus plans, the final version of the American Recovery and Reinvestment Act (ARRA) included both spending measures and tax cuts. The spending measures accounted for about two-thirds of the program's $787 billion cost, with taxcuts accounting for the remaining one-third. Some of the spending was intended to put people back to work directly on infrastructure and other public works projects. Assistance was given to people hit hard by the recession in the form of aid for health care costs, unemployment compensation, education, job training, and food assistance. Spending also included investment in renewable energy and science. Nearly $1.5 billion was allocated to state and local governments, which were also impacted by the recession.

Economic Policy Gridlock

Stimulus plans generally yield mixed success. Even the New Deal, the most famous of all stimulus packages, is not usually credited with fully reviving the economy and pulling America out of the Great Depression. The New Deal put millions of people to work and created many worthy programs, but the economy did not regain its full strength until the country began mobilization for World War II.

In order to be effective, a stimulus plan must be large enough to make a difference in the economy. It must also be timely. For example, a stimulus plan designed to combat a 1975 recession was still under discussion in 1977, long after its implememtation would be of any use and after the worst of the crisis had already passed.

Cash for Clunkers proved so popular that its $1 billion appropriation was tripled. The stimulus measure was intended to boost car sales and support the auto industry.

Congress planned that most ARRA spending would be distributed throughout 2009 and 2010, with funds tapering off in 2011. In the months and years after the stimulus plan was enacted, Americans began seeing road signs announcing that highway construction and improvement projects had been funded by ARRA. Some programs—such as Cash for Clunkers, which encouraged people to trade in older vehicles for new models with better gas mileage—were high-profile and popular. Other measures, such as a tax cut that affected nearly all working families, went largely unnoticed.

As the stimulus measures wound down, high unemployment numbers persisted. Republicans declared that the stimulus plan had been a failure. The Obama administration and many economists pointed out that the plan had succeeded in saving jobs and the economy would have deteriorated further without intervention. Nevertheless, the stimulus package failed to produce the strong recovery that many Americans had hoped to see.

Policymakers wrestled with the next course of action. Some economists and lawmakers believed that the stimulus plan had been too small and the situation called for more aggressive spending. This was the minority viewpoint, however, especially after the 2010 elections gave Republicans a majority in the House. Many new representatives strongly advocated spending cuts to balance the budget, rather than continued stimulus measures that would add to the ballooning budget deficit and national debt.

The Republican stance is based on the position that it is irresponsible for the American government to increase the national debt. When the government spends more than it brings in through taxes, it has to borrow money. The debt will eventually have to be paid off, and annual interest payments on the debt add to the government's expenses. According to this viewpoint, the huge national debt is a hazard that could devastate the economy. To avoid this danger, spending should be sharply reined in to balance the budget and begin paying down debt. According to the opposing viewpoint, deep spending cuts would cripple programs essential for the nation's continued prosperity and starve the economy of cash at the exact moment when it is needed most.

As debate has grown more contentious, discussions in Congress have become heated and resistant to compromise. Substantial spending measures, such as a proposed stimulus measure in 2011, were blocked. There were fierce arguments over measures such as a payroll tax cut renewal, an extension of unemployment benefits, a jobs bill, and raising the federal debt limit. A battle over the nation's budget nearly led to a government shutdown. As the health of the economy continues to remain uncertain and the national debt continues to grow, it is likely that the partisan strife will continue.

Chapter 3

Economic Consequences for States, Businesses, and Communities

During a recession, government and private enterprises bring in less revenue than they need to keep programs and services running. This creates additional stress on the economy, as more people are in need of help during times of economic hardship. Private businesses make less money, meaning that governments get less tax revenue to spend on programs that people need. Governments are often forced to choose between providing basic services, giving emergency aid to those suffering in the weak economy, and fulfilling existing financial obligations.

For communities, a recession can mean the loss of employment as businesses cut workers or close down. During the Great Recession, many communities saw a rise in vacant properties as banks foreclosed on homes and financial institutions were reluctant to make new loans to potential homebuyers. Local governments and charitable

A food bank in Wilmington, Ohio, saw demand rise sharply after the shipping company DHL laid off thousands of workers, sending the local economy reeling.

organizations saw an increase in demand for services as funding and donations declined.

Economic Indicators

During a recession, the way people use money often changes dramatically. Employers may have to cut worker pay or hours in order to stay in business. Employees may be laid off or expected to perform at a higher level with the same or even less pay than before. People spend less money because less is available. Retailers may cut the price of expensive merchandise to move it off the shelves at a time when few people are buying. The cost of other products may go up because of increases in the cost of transportation.

Economists watch what's going on and compile data based on trending changes in the economy. The statistics they put together are called economic indicators, and they are used to determine economic conditions. These statistics enable economists to analyze current and recent economic performance and predict how the economy will perform in the future. They give economists an idea of the general health of the economy and help them chart periods of expansion or contraction.

Economic indicators are classified into three categories according to the timing of their appearance in the business cycle: leading indicators, lagging indicators, and coincident indicators. Leading indicators usually change before the economy as a whole changes. They are the numbers that typically grab headlines when they begin changing for better or for worse. Leading indicators can be volatile, and economists usually wait for them to move in one direction for several months before predicting a change in the business cycle.

Stock prices are one example of a leading indicator. The stock market often begins a decline before the rest of the economy starts slumping, then starts rebounding before the rest of the economy starts recovering. The number of new building permits issued is another leading indicator. Construction falls off during recessions, when credit becomes tighter and people don't feel as financially secure. Initial jobless claims represent the number of workers seeking unemployment benefits. Drops in the number of initial jobless claims filed can indicate that employers are starting to hire again.

Lagging indicators usually change after the economy has turned a corner. The lag can be as long as several months. Lagging indicators can't be used to predict how the economy will perform because they aren't measured until after the economy has already shifted upward or downward. Instead, economists use them to confirm that a trend has indeed developed and new economic conditions have taken hold.

One of the most widely used lagging indicators is the unemployment rate, which measures the number of people who are looking for work within a set period. If the unemployment rate is rising, it indicates that businesses have stopped hiring and are cutting employees, which is an indication that the economy is performing poorly. For workers who have lost their jobs, it means that they may have a harder time finding a new job, while those who remain employed may be less likely to change jobs.

During economic hard times, taking advantage of coupons and any other kinds of discounts and store sales can be a crucial means of financial survival.

Coincident indicators are indicators that change at the same time that the business cycle changes. They can be used to confirm economic health and identify economic weak spots. Personal income is a commonly used coincident indicator. When the economy is strong, personal income generally goes up. But when the economy starts to struggle, personal income may fall or remain flat. Likewise, industrial production, manufacturing, and trade sales increase in a strong economy and fall in a weak one.

Pinching Pennies and Slashing Services

State and local governments experience budget shortfalls during recessions. Since people are making less money, governments are not able to take in as much in taxes as when the economy is strong. Further stress is placed on government budgets during recessions by increased demand for public services, as more people have to seek assistance from government programs in order to make ends meet. Making matters worse, the federal government may reduce aid to states during a recession. States, in turn, cut back on funding for local government programs that are often already cash-strapped. Many states have spending deficits, meaning they spend more than they collect through taxes and other revenue.

As the economy recovered from the Great Recession, state and local governments were pressured to balance their budgets. Forty-nine of the fifty states have laws requiring a balanced budget. Vermont is the only exception. To achieve a balanced budget when tax revenues remain low, states have to cut spending. Lawmakers often try to spread budget cuts broadly so that the cuts aren't all made in one place. But programs that were already lacking adequate funding often have to take drastic measures in order to remain in operation. For example, state-funded mental health centers may have to cut their program offerings or lay off staff so that they can remain open to serve people in need.

The Great Recession that began in 2007 produced the greatest dropoff in state revenues in U.S. history. According to a study by the Center on Budget and Policy Priorities, thirty states have projected budget shortfalls totaling $49 million for the 2013 fiscal year. At the same time, states expect to see their education and health care obligations continue to grow.

The study also found that states expect to educate 350,000 more students in kindergarten through the twelfth grade and 1.7 million more public college and university students in 2012–13 than in 2007–08. In addition, 5.6 million more people are expected to be eligible for health care through Medicaid in 2012 than were enrolled in the program before the recession began.

During a recession, many different services may be cut as governments try to stretch funds as far as possible. A transit agency may have to cut some of its less-used bus routes or cut back on the hours that buses run. Libraries may cut back on the hours they are open. They may have to cut back on their programs and lay off librarians. Public health programs may suffer; their funding may be reduced at the precise time when more people need inexpensive health care.

The effects of a recession on education can be seen throughout the school day. At school, you may notice that

CHICAGO
PUBLIC LIBRARY

La Biblioteca Pública de
Chicago
estará cerrada el lunes
17 de agosto, 2009.

The Chicago Public Library
will be closed on
Monday, August 17, 2009.

FREE
WiFi

...r learns that the Chicago Public Library
...ed due to a furlough day intended to
...alance the budget. City employees
...ithout pay for the day.

classrooms are more crowded because there are fewer teachers. Public schools may also have more students because parents who once sent their children to private schools can no longer afford to do so. There may be fewer afterschool programs and sports offered. Books, computers, lab equipment, and other school supplies may be old

Hard Times for States

The Great Recession caused economic woe across the nation, but some states were hit harder than others. Midwestern states, particularly Michigan, experienced severe downturns due to the crisis in the auto industry and the general slump in manufacturing. In 2009, Michigan saw unemployment levels over 14 percent, the highest in the country. States that prospered during the housing boom also experienced heavier job losses and deeper economic pain. These included California, Arizona, Nevada, and Florida. Once the economy started adding jobs again, however, states that suffered the most began rebounding faster than others.

A few states, especially those with strong revenue from energy resources, managed to escape the worst effects of the recession. Oil-rich North Dakota, in particular, barely noticed the economic downturn. At the height of the recession, unemployment levels peaked there at 4.2 percent. While many states were shedding jobs, North Dakota added so many jobs that it often had trouble attracting qualified workers.

or out of date because the school district can't afford to buy new materials.

Basic services offered by towns and cities may change. Garbage may be picked up less often than before. Potholes may not be patched as quickly, and streetlights that go out may not be fixed as promptly. Local governments may start charging more for services. People may see their water bills go up, or they may have to pay higher fees for community programs. It may cost more to take a train or a bus across town because of fare hikes that were needed to make up for cuts to public transportation funding.

Unemployment Woes

Early in the Great Recession, the unemployment level had been projected to peak at 8.5 percent before beginning to fall. Instead, it kept climbing until it peaked at about 10.1 percent in October 2009. Even as the economy showed signs of recovery, unemployment remained stubbornly high, staying above 9 percent until November 2011. The unemployment rate does not count underemployed workers, such as part-time workers who would prefer a full-time job.

Unemployment figures rise during recessions because corporations experience a drop in demand for their products and services. They cut jobs and lay off workers in order to offset their losses and remain viable. Some business sectors are hit harder than others. People often hold off on making big purchases or investments until they see evidence that the economy is improving.

The auto, construction, and banking industries were hit particularly hard by the Great Recession. Construction jobs were lost because people couldn't secure the financing to build new homes. Carmakers saw such dramatic drops in sales that U.S. automakers General Motors and Chrysler were both forced to declare bankruptcy, while Ford had to restructure its debt. All three survived the crisis, but not before thousands of jobs were lost in areas ranging from parts manufacturing to sales. The banking industry shed jobs as hundreds of banks closed and were taken over by other financial institutions. Other banks cut employees in order to streamline operations and stay afloat.

With high unemployment, job insecurity, and pay cuts, people become more careful about their spending. Instead

Weeds grow in front of an empty car dealership in Nashville, Tennessee. As part of their reorganization following bankruptcy, auto manufacturers closed thousands of dealerships nationwide.

of buying new merchandise, they may opt for used or refurbished items, such as computers, appliances, or power tools. They may skip appointments they ordinarily would have kept, such as dentist appointments or visits to a hair salon, in order to save money. These cutbacks can have a ripple effect on small businesses that depend on regular customers and can worsen the economic pressures on their owners. To stay open, they may have to cut back on their hours or lay off workers.

Although the economy began adding jobs during the recovery from the Great Recession, the overall unemployment rate dropped relatively slowly. One reason is that unemployment figures do not count discouraged workers who have given up on searching for a job. As job prospects improve, discouraged workers begin seeking work again and are added once more to the unemployment statistics until they find a job or stop looking.

Chapter 4
Coping with Tough Times at Home

According to the standard business cycle model, a period of recession is followed by a recovery and a return to economic growth. Looking at the graph, you might reasonably conclude that life returns to "normal" during the recovery. In the real world, however, the scenario is not so straightforward.

After a recession, it takes years for the economy to regain prerecession levels of employment. For the past few decades, the recovery period for the labor market has been longer with each recession. After the 1973 recession, it took twenty-four months for employment to recover. After the 1981 and 1990 recessions, it took twenty-eight and thirty-one months, respectively. After the 2001 recession, employment recovered after forty-seven months—nearly four years. The Great Recession officially ended in June 2009, but in early 2012, employment levels were still 5 percent below prerecession levels.

In addition, Americans had invested much of their savings in their homes during the years leading up to the recession. Much of this money was lost forever in the housing bust, leaving people financially strapped. Economic recoveries generally depend on consumers starting to spend again. In the aftermath of the Great Recession, many people do not have the means to do so.

When Money's Tight

Consumer spending is one of the main factors driving the American economy. About 70 percent of the nation's GDP is the result of people buying "stuff"—from food and toys to refrigerators and cars. In a healthy economy, people feel confident enough about their economic position that they spend money on goods and services. During an

A woman pushes a cartful of groceries received from a Los Angeles, California, food bank. The recession saw a sharp increase in demand for food aid.

economic downturn, however, money is tight and people are wary of their economic future. People skimp and save, rather than spend freely.

During a recession, people examine their daily lives looking for new ways to save money. Instead of buying name-brand grocery products, they purchase a cheaper store brand. They start clipping coupons and eating at restaurants less often. People may try planting gardens for the first time and freezing or canning extra produce. For back-to-school shopping, parents might shop at stores with cheaper prices and buy fewer clothes than last year. Instead of flying to Disney World for a vacation, the family might take a road trip to a nearby attraction.

Consumers often delay major purchases during a recession. People may put off buying a new washing machine or a car, for example, until the economy begins to improve. During the Great Recession, prices of used cars spiked because of high demand.

For most people, this period of insecurity ends once a recovery is underway. For some families, however, the recession takes a deeper toll. Losing a job or taking a pay cut can cause significant financial hardship. People may end up living paycheck-to-paycheck and resort to depleting their savings to pay bills. They may even take out small loans at extremely high interest rates in order to meet expenses. Some families apply to the government for food stamps or turn to a food bank for help. The Great Recession saw a huge increase in demand at food banks, with some organizations reporting increases of 150 percent or more in user demand over prerecession levels.

During the Great Recession, the drop in consumer spending was abrupt and shocking. The financial crisis reached its most critical point in the autumn and winter of 2008 during the Christmas shopping season. Retailers reported the worst holiday sales since 1970, with many stores seeing a 10 percent or more drop from 2007.

Tough Times for Young and Old

A recession does not affect all demographic groups equally. During the Great Recession, many of the jobs lost were in male-dominated areas, such as construction and industry. More men than women lost their jobs during the recession. Once the economy began adding jobs, however, unemployment levels fell more quickly among men than women.

Younger workers, especially those entering the job market for the first time, tend to fare worse during recessions than experienced workers. During a recession, newly hired workers begin at a lower pay rate than during prosperous times. The wage gap persists after the recession ends. Studies have shown that years later, these workers still earn less than workers hired during a thriving economic climate.

Today, the effects of the recession linger for younger adults who face high unemployment numbers and a tough job market. In 2012, employment among workers under thirty-four was at the lowest level since the 1980s. Many college graduates are deep in debt from student loans. They may take low-paying, entry-level jobs or unpaid internships upon graduation. Crunched for money, an increasing number of twentysomethings are moving back home with their parents. Almost half of all unemployed young people moved in with their parents at least temporarily. Multigenerational households have become

Protesters in New York City rally against tuition increases. The high price of a college education leaves many students with substantial levels of student loan debt upon graduating.

a safety net for young people. Most young adults have a friend or family member who has moved back home due to the economy, and the practice is becoming more socially acceptable.

Young Americans are also waiting longer to marry and have children than in the past. Today, people tend to wait to marry until they are well-set financially—an uncertain prospect in the aftermath of the recession. Studies have shown that women have fewer babies in a troubled economy. During the first decade of the twenty-first century, the birth rate peaked in 2007 and then fell sharply.

The effects of a recession hurt children as well. After 2007, the number of children living in poverty increased drastically. One study found that the Great Recession completely erased thirty-five years of economic improvement for families with children. Many children saw a parent lose a job or take a pay cut, and many families became reliant on food stamps. The number of homeless families and children rose during the recession, and cases of domestic violence increased. In addition, government investment in programs offering services for children declined. The long-term impact of the recession on children is impossible to predict. Children thrive best in a stable home environment, and the recession caused upheaval in many families.

Older workers are particularly vulnerable to the economic toll of a recession. Unlike younger workers, they might not have time to regain financial stability as the recovery strengthens.

Economic hardship resulting from the recession forced many Americans into poverty and even homelessness. Here, a family of six lives in a Tennessee campground for $325 a month.

The Great Recession saw a drastic loss of wealth and savings. Many older adults had to resort to withdrawing money from their retirement savings during the financial downturn. Many have delayed retirement or have come out of retirement due to economic conditions. Older workers were less likely to lose their jobs, but unemployed older workers had a harder time finding new jobs.

Minorities were disproportionately impacted by the Great Recession. Overall, unemployment numbers fell to 8.2 percent by early 2012. Unemployment levels for black and Hispanic workers, however, remained in the double digits. Minority groups also suffered greater relative financial losses due to the economic downturn. On average, black and Hispanic households lost more than 50 percent of their wealth over the course of the recession, mostly because of the decline in home values. This has led to record-high gaps in wealth between white and minority households.

Losing the House

Every recession leaves behind financial losses and the disruption of lives and livelihoods. The Great Recession was exceptionally long and severe. It differed from prior recessions in one other significant way. For the first time since the Great Depression, millions of Americans lost their homes.

During the boom years, rates of home ownership soared. The economy soured when many borrowers could not pay back their expensive mortgages with high interest rates. The ensuing financial crisis and recession further hurt borrowers' ability to repay their loans, and more

The Pain of Long-Term Unemployment

The Great Recession produced levels of long-term unemployment not seen since the Great Depression. In early 2012, 5.3 million people had been unemployed for twenty-seven weeks or longer. These long-term unemployed people represented over 40 percent of the total number of unemployed Americans. Many of them measured their span of unemployment in months or even years, not weeks.

For unemployed workers, it often becomes difficult as the months pass by to maintain contacts in their job field and keep job skills up-to-date for a rapidly changing workplace. The long-term unemployed are more likely than the short-term unemployed to settle for jobs that are less satisfactory than their old jobs or abandon their field altogether to pursue a new career.

Long-term unemployment often causes considerable financial difficulty, but research has shown that it also has serious health effects. Unemployment undermines relationships and creates a loss of self-respect and self-esteem. Long-term unemployed workers are more likely to suffer from mental and physical health problems, especially depression. According to one study, an extended period of unemployment measurably decreases life expectancy.

people defaulted, or failed to make required payments on their home loans.

Before the recession, people could often sell their homes quickly and make a huge profit. After the financial crisis, the market for real estate collapsed, and the number of homes for sale increased due to foreclosures. There were no buyers for homes, and home values plummeted. In many cases, due to this decline in value, homeowners ended up owing more money to the bank in loans than what their house was actually worth. They still had to repay the loans, even if it caused financial difficulties. Many homeowners wanted to move and escape their "underwater"

New York State's mobile Foreclosure Relief Unit offers information on loan modification to homeowners in danger of losing their homes.

mortgages, as they were called. Even if owners could find a buyer, they would lose money selling the house.

Throughout the recession, the government attempted to institute programs to help struggling homeowners, with little success. The foreclosure crisis was a complex and hugely expensive issue. Negative equity for mortgages—the amount that they are underwater—totaled about $700 billion in early 2012. The attitude of the banks further complicated efforts to offer relief for homeowners. On one hand, banks wanted to resolve the foreclosure crisis so that the housing market could recover. On the other hand, they did not want to write off the value of loans, even for borrowers with underwater mortgages, and lose money as a result.

The foreclosure crisis led to families being forced out of their homes, sometimes into homelessness. Some home-owners, unable to pay legal fees, were evicted from their homes despite suspecting wrongful foreclosures on the part of banks. Even pets became innocent victims as people los-ing their homes were unable to keep them and either gave them away or abandoned them. The effects of the crisis went beyond individual homeowners. In communities with high foreclosure rates, property values in entire neighborhoods were dragged down. Renters saw their rents rise because of higher demand. The economy as a whole suffered as a result of an unstable housing market, which was one of the biggest obstacles to an economic recovery.

Chapter 5
Economic Recovery and Beyond

Even after a recession ends, many people struggle economically before they see a return to prosperity. They may not consider the crisis over until they have seen a difference in their own lives, such as finding a new job, seeing their pay increase, or finally being able to sell their home at a profit. People often remain wary about the economy for some time. They may save more of their earnings or continue to cut back on unnecessary expenses. It may be a while before they spend money at prerecession levels.

Economic indicators may take some time to reflect the changing economy. After the Great Recession ended, for example, unemployment remained above 9 percent for months and was still above 8 percent as of early 2012, with little chance of falling to prerecession levels for years to come. The housing market remained stagnant, with sales lagging in many parts of the country and home prices far below prerecession levels.

A man passes by a row of empty commercial spaces and signs advertising sales and steep discounts. Years after the recession officially ended, uncertain economic conditions continued to affect businesses and individuals alike.

States and communities also may continue to struggle after the recession ends. Lawmakers may remain under pressure to reign in spending on government programs and projects. Communities also may be slow to recover from a recession. Businesses that were forced to close during an economic downturn often do not reopen. It may be years before vacant stores and factories are occupied again. Neighborhoods may have to deal with foreclosed homes that have been left empty. Schools may take a while to get the funding to update equipment and hire more teachers.

Return to Economic Growth

A recession is officially over when GDP growth is positive again. Often, several months may pass after the first indications of GDP growth before economists announce the end of a recession. By that time, multiple economic indicators may show the economy improving. These may include strong stock market figures, increased factory orders, and shrinking unemployment figures.

However, not all economic indicators improve when a recovery begins. The Great Recession officially ended in June 2009. Many economic indicators pointed to a recovery, including improved manufacturing data and the rise of stock prices. But the unemployment rate remained high, and the economy actually shed about nine hundred thousand workers in the first nine months of the recovery. The housing market also remained unsteady. While home sales showed signs of recovering in some areas, they stayed sluggish in others, and home prices in general remained far lower than prerecession levels.

Aftereffects of a Recession

During and after a recession, many people are anxious to find a root cause for the economic downturn or someone they can blame. Individuals may blame government spending, shady business and banking practices, or an economic bubble. Even when several factors may contribute to a recession, a root cause is often identified and targeted. People often demand reforms intended to keep the same conditions from occurring in the future. Lawmakers may hold hearings on

Surrounded by members of Congress, President Barack Obama signs the Dodd-Frank Wall Street Reform and Consumer Protection financial overhaul bill into law.

the recession's cause and pass legislation meant to protect the nation's economy. Some may point to too much regulation as the cause of a recession, while others may say that more rules and government oversight are needed to prevent a recurrence.

In the immediate aftermath of the Great Depression, several reforms were put into place to guarantee that such an event would not happen again. The Banking Act of 1933 created the FDIC and imposed several banking reforms. The act increased the power of the Federal Reserve Board to regulate banking, separated commercial banking from investment banking, and established a temporary FDIC, which became permanent in 1935. Some aspects of the bill remain in effect more than seventy years later, though banks long argued that the act limited their competitiveness with international banks, and some elements of the law have been repealed as a result.

After the Great Recession, Congress passed the Dodd-Frank Wall Street Reform and Consumer Protection Act in June 2010. The 2,300-page law affects nearly every aspect of the financial services industry and reverses nearly three decades of financial deregulation. The bill created the Bureau of Consumer Financial Protection within the Federal Reserve to protect consumers in the financial marketplace. It also established a council of monitors to watch the financial markets for major risks, and it gave the government the power to seize and dismantle troubled financial institutions whose failure would hurt the economy. Many lawmakers were dissatisfied with the bill, saying it would damage the economy through overregulation and would be too costly to implement. Others said it did not go far enough.

Paying for Oil Dependence

The 1970s was a decade dominated by a phenomenon that economists dubbed "stagflation"—stagnant growth combined with high inflation. The decade began with a recession that had started in late 1969 and ended in late 1970. Another recession, this time long and deep, began in 1973 and lasted until 1975. After the recovery, events of 1979 produced another recession that extended through the first half of 1980.

One root cause of the mid-1970s recession was a sudden quadrupling of oil prices. Oil-producing countries in the Middle East embargoed the United States for political reasons during 1973–74, which reduced the supply of oil. Another disruption in the oil supply occurred in 1979, when a revolution in Iran interrupted production.

Over three decades later, the United States is still highly dependent on foreign oil. During the 2000s, oil prices spiked and reached a record-high level in mid-2008. Many observers predicted that continuing high oil prices would drag the economy down. Instead, oil prices fell drastically as a result of the financial crisis and recession. When prices began rising again in 2011 and 2012, people once again began predicting dire consequences, especially given the fragile nature of the postrecession recovery.

Debating the National Debt

The end of the Great Recession was marked by calls to deal with the ballooning national debt. As of April 2012, the national debt stood at about $15.6 trillion, almost triple the debt that existed in 2000. Many critics believe that excessive government spending endangers the nation's economy. In the long-term future, annual interest payments on the national debt will total hundreds of billions of dollars. These payments will become even more costly as interest rates rise and could potentially hinder economic growth. Others argue that stimulus spending and bailouts were needed to save the economy from a much greater financial catastrophe. Deficits are undesirable but necessary, and the long-term growth made possible through government intervention during the downturn will

The National Debt Clock in New York City displays the figure of the continually increasing national debt, even as Congress formally raised the debt limit in 2011.

allow the economy to eventually overcome the issue of the national debt.

The debate over the debt neared a crisis point in 2011, as Congress debated raising the limit on how much money the government could borrow and pushed the nation to the brink of defaulting on its debts. In August 2011, the credit rating agency Standard & Poor's downgraded the nation's bond rating—which measures how likely the rating institution thinks it is that the government can pay its debts—for the first time in history. The lower bond rating could mean the nation will have to pay even higher interest rates on money borrowed in the future.

Some lawmakers who see the debt as an immediate threat to the economy seek to balance the federal budget through cuts in government spending. Many of these cuts would come through the elimination of government departments, layers of bureaucracy, and social programs. Critics of such austerity measures claim that these cuts would actually harm the economy by gutting programs that are essential for many Americans.

Looking to the Future

It is hard to say how long it might take for the economy to fully recover from a recession. In recent times, each recovery has taken longer than previous recoveries. The same is true for predicting when the next recession might occur. While recessions are a normal part of the business cycle, it is hard to chart when the economy might be peaking before it starts to decline. Recessions also vary in duration and severity. Some may be relatively short and mild, while

British public sector workers in London strike to protest government austerity measures that slashed public spending, which led to job losses and reduced benefits.

others—like the Great Recession—take years to resolve. You may continue to hear about the effects of the Great Recession for some time.

Economists often try to predict what the next economic bubble might be and come up with solutions for avoiding the coming crisis. Many of these predictions turn out to be wrong. At other times, their dire warnings and gloomy predictions may go unheard as the nation heads toward another recession.

While legislation and regulations aimed at preventing a recurrence of the Great Recession have gone into effect, it is too early to know the full impact the new laws might have on the economy in the future. Economic forces are too complex to preempt an economic downturn. It is very difficult to predict economic trends beyond the short term. Economists can hope the economy remains strong as it recovers and any economic rough patches can be overcome quickly and without too much strain.

bankruptcy The legal process in which a person or group declares an inability to pay debts.

budget A summary, often itemized, of expected revenue and expenditures for a given period.

business cycle Alternating periods of growth and contraction in the economy.

central bank An institution or agency, either associated with the government or independent, that is responsible for exercising control of a nation's monetary and financial systems.

consumer A person or organization that uses economic goods, especially for personal rather than commercial use.

credit An arrangement to use or possess goods or services on condition of later payment.

debt Something that is owed or that one is bound to pay to or perform for another.

demand The amount of a good or service that consumers will buy at a given price.

fiscal Related to the use of government spending and taxing powers.

foreclosure The legal proceedings taken by a creditor to repossess a mortgaged property, as when loan payments have not been made.

gross domestic product (GDP) The value of all goods and services produced in a nation during a period of time, usually a year.

inflation An increase in general price levels of goods and services.

interest A sum paid or charged for the use of money or for borrowing money, often expressed as a percentage of money borrowed and to be paid back within a given time period.

investment Money committed in order to earn a future financial return.

mortgage A pledge of property, such as a house, as security for a loan to be repaid under specific terms.

profit Money left to a producer or employer after costs such as wages, rent, and raw materials are paid.

recession An economic downturn in the business cycle, usually defined as six months or more of declining GDP.

recovery The upward phase of the business cycle in which economic conditions improve.

stimulus In economics, government-initiated measures intended to spur growth.

stock Ownership shares of a company or corporation.

FOR MORE INFORMATION

Bank of Canada
234 Wellington Street
Ottawa, ON K1A 0G9
Canada
(800) 303-1282
Web site: http://www.bankofcanada.ca
The Bank of Canada is the central bank of Canada.

Board of Governors of the Federal Reserve System
20th Street and Constitution Avenue NW
Washington, DC 20551
Web site: http://www.federalreserve.gov
The Federal Reserve is the central bank of the United States.

Committee for a Responsible Federal Budget Project
1899 L Street NW, Suite 400
Washington, DC 20036
(202) 986-6599
Web site: http://stimulus.org
Run by a bipartisan, nonrofit organization, this committee
    tracks stimulus funds and other government spending
    implemented to address the 2007 recession.

Department of Finance Canada
140 O'Connor Street
Ottawa, ON K1A 0G5
Canada
(613) 992-1573

Web site: http://www.fin.gc.ca
The Department of Finance oversees the Canadian
  government's budget and spending.

Federal Deposit Insurance Corporation (FDIC)
Public Information Center
3501 North Fairfax Drive
Arlington, VA 22226
(877) 275-3342
Web site: http://www.fdic.gov
The Federal Deposit Insurance Corporation is the
  government agency that insures bank deposits.

Federal Housing Administration (FHA)
U.S. Department of Housing and Urban Development
451 7th Street SW
Washington, DC 20410
(202) 708-1112
Web site: http://portal.hud.gov/hudportal/HUD?src=/
  program_offices/housing/fhahistory
The Federal Housing Administration, generally known as
  FHA, provides mortgage insurance on loans made by
  FHA-approved lenders throughout the United States
  and its territories. FHA insures mortgages on single
  family and multifamily homes, including manufactured
  homes and hospitals. It is the largest insurer of mortgages in the world, insuring over thirty-four million
  properties since its inception in 1934.

National Economists Club
P.O. Box 19281
Washington, DC 20036
(703) 493-8824
Web site: http://www.national-economists.org
This nonprofit, nonpartisan organization has the goal of
    encouraging and sponsoring discussion and an exchange
    of ideas on economic trends, issues, and public policy.

U.S. Department of the Treasury
1500 Pennsylvania Avenue NW
Washington, DC 20220
(202) 622-2000
Web site: http://www.treas.gov
The Treasury's mission is to maintain a strong economy and
    create economic and job opportunities by promoting the
    conditions that enable economic growth and stability at
    home and abroad, strengthen national security by combat-
    ing threats and protecting the integrity of the financial
    system, and manage the U.S. government's finances and
    resources effectively.

Web Sites

Due to the changing nature of Internet links, Rosen Publishing
has developed an online list of Web sites related to the sub-
ject of this book. This site is updated regularly. Please use
this link to access the list:
http://www.rosenlinks.com/YEF/Rece

FOR FURTHER READING

Acton, Johnny, and David Goldblatt. *Economy*. New York, NY: DK, 2010.

Berlatsky, Noah, ed. *The Global Financial Crisis* (Global Viewpoints). San Diego, CA: Greenhaven Press, 2010.

Brancato, Robin F. *Money: Getting It, Using It, and Avoiding the Traps* (The Ultimate Teen Guide). Lanham, MD: Scarecrow Press, 2007.

Clifford, Tim. *Our Economy in Action*. Vero Beach, FL: Rourke Publishing, 2009.

Clinton, Bill. *Back to Work: Why We Need Smart Government for a Strong Economy*. New York, NY: Alfred A. Knopf, 2011.

Cohen, Jeff. *The Complete Idiot's Guide to Recession-Proof Careers*. New York, NY: Alpha, 2010.

Craats, Rennay. *Economy: USA Past Present Future*. New York, NY: Weigl Publishers, 2009.

Day, Vox. *The Return of the Great Depression*. Los Angeles, CA: WND Books, 2009.

Espejo, Roman. *The American Housing Crisis* (At Issue). San Diego, CA: Greenhaven Press, 2009.

Flynn, Sean Masaki. *Economics for Dummies*. Hoboken, NJ: Wiley, 2011.

Friedman, Thomas L., and Michael Mandelbaum. *That Used to Be Us: How America Fell Behind in the World It Invented and How We Can Come Back*. New York, NY: Farrar, Straus and Giroux, 2011.

Galbraith, John Kenneth. *The Great Crash of 1929*. New York, NY: Mariner Books, 2009.

Gross, Daniel. *Dumb Money: How Our Greatest Financial Minds Bankrupted the Nation.* New York, NY: Free Press, 2009.

Hall, Alvin. *Show Me the Money: How to Make Cents of Economics.* New York, NY: DK, 2008.

Heinrichs, Ann. *The Great Recession* (Cornerstones of Freedom). New York, NY: Children's Press, 2011.

Hynson, Colin. *The Credit Crunch* (The World Today). North Mankato, MN: Sea to Sea Publications, 2010.

Mayer, David A. *The Everything Economics Book: From Theory to Practice, Your Complete Guide to Understanding Economics Today.* Avon, MA: Adams Media, 2010.

Merino, Noel. *The World Economy* (Current Controversies). San Diego, CA: Greenhaven Press, 2010.

Miller Debra A. *The U.S. Economy* (Current Controversies). San Diego, CA: Greenhaven Press, 2010.

Nagle, Jeanne. *How a Recession Works* (Real World Economics). New York, NY: Rosen Publishing, 2009.

Orr, Tamra. *A Kid's Guide to Stock Market Investing.* Hockessin, DE: Mitchell Lane Publishers, 2009.

Rauchway, Eric. *The Great Depression and the New Deal: A Very Short Introduction.* New York, NY: Oxford University Press, 2008.

Riggs, Thomas, ed. *Everyday Finance: Economics, Personal Money Management, and Entrepreneurship.* Detroit, MI: Gale Group, 2008.

Rosenberg, Jerry Martin. *The Concise Encyclopedia of the Great Recession, 2007–2010.* Lanham, MD: Scarecrow Press, 2010.

Shlaes, Amity. *The Forgotten Man: A New History of the Great Depression.* New York, NY: Harper Perennial, 2008.

Tucker, Irvin. *Economics for Today.* 3rd ed. Mason, OH: Thomson Learning, 2003.

Tyson, Eric. *Investing for Dummies.* 5th ed. Hoboken, NJ: Wiley, 2008.

Wasik, John F. *The Audacity of Help: Obama's Economic Plan and the Remaking of America.* New York, NY: Bloomberg Press, 2009.

Watkins, T.H. *The Great Depression: America in the 1930s.* New York, NY: Back Bay Books, 2009.

Whitcraft, Melissa. *Wall Street* (Cornerstones of Freedom). New York, NY: Children's Press, 2008.

BIBLIOGRAPHY

Barr, Tracy L. *Living Well in a Down Economy for Dummies.*
   Hoboken, NJ: Wiley, 2008.

Bivens, Josh. *Failure by Design: The Story Behind America's
   Broken Economy.* Ithaca, NY: ILR Press, 2011.

Bureau of Labor Statistics. "Employment Situation
   Summary." April 6, 2012. Retrieved April 2012 (http://
   www.bls.gov/news.release/empsit.nr0.htm).

Congressional Budget Office. "Understanding and
   Responding to Persistently High Unemployment."
   February 16, 2012. Retrieved April 2012 (http://www
   .cbo.gov/publication/42989).

Demos.org. "The State of Young America: Economic
   Barriers to the American Dream." Retrieved April 2012
   (http://www.demos.org/state-of-young-america).

Economist. "The Recession: When Did It End?" April 15,
   2010. Retrieved April 2012 (http://www.economist.
   com/node/15911334).

Epping, Randy Charles. *The 21st Century Economy: A
   Beginner's Guide.* New York, NY: Vintage Books, 2009.

Gordon, John Steele. *An Empire of Wealth: The Epic
   History of American Economic Power.* New York, NY:
   HarperCollins, 2004.

Gorman, Tom. *The Complete Idiot's Guide to the Great
   Recession.* New York, NY: Alpha Books, 2010.

Kochhar, Rakesh, and D'Vera Cohn. "Fighting Poverty in a
   Bad Economy, Americans Move in with Relatives." Pew
   Research Center, October 3, 2011. Retrieved April 2012
   (http://www.pewsocialtrends.org/2011/10/03/

fighting-poverty-in-a-bad-economy-americans-move-in-with-relatives/?src-prc-headline).

Kochhar, Rakesh, et al. "Wealth Gaps Rise to Record Highs Between Whites, Blacks, Hispanics Twenty-to-One." Pew Research Center, July 26, 2011. Retrieved April 2012 (http://www.pewsocialtrends. org/2011/07/26/wealth-gaps-rise-to-record-highs -between-whites-blacks-hispanics).

Land, Kenneth C. "2011 Child and Youth Well-Being Index (CWI)." Foundation for Child Development, November 14, 2011. Retrieved April 2012 (http://fcd-us.org/sites/ default/files/FINAL%20CWI%20Report.pdf).

Livingston, Gretchen. "In a Down Economy, Fewer Births." Pew Research Center, October 12, 2011. Retrieved April 2012 (http://www.pewsocialtrends.org/2011/10/12/ in-a-down-economy-fewer-births/?src=prc-headline).

Lyall, Sarah, and Alan Cowell. "Britons Strike as Government Extends Austerity Measures." *New York Times,* November 30, 2011. Retrieved April 2012 (http://www.nytimes .com/2011/12/01/world/europe/great-britain-strike -austerity-measures.html).

Mason, Paul. *Meltdown: The End of the Age of Greed.* New York, NY: Verso, 2009.

National Bureau of Economic Research. "U.S. Business Cycle Expansions and Contractions." Retrieved April 2012 (http://www.nber.org/cycles.html).

New York Times. "Economic Crisis and Market Upheavals." October 3, 2011. Retrieved April 2012 (http://topics

.nytimes.com/top/reference/timestopics/subjects/c/
credit_crisis/index.html).

New York Times. "Economic Stimulus—Jobs Bills." March
15, 2012. Retrieved April 2012 (http://topics.nytimes.
com/top/reference/timestopics/subjects/u/united_
states_economy/economic_stimulus/index.html).

New York Times. "Federal Budget." April 19, 2012. Retrieved
April 2012 (http://topics.nytimes.com/top/reference/
timestopics/subjects/f/federal_budget_us/index.html).

New York Times. "Foreclosures." April 2, 2012. Retrieved
April 2012 (http://topics.nytimes.com/top/reference/
timestopics/subjects/f/foreclosures/index.html).

Parker, Kim. "The Boomerang Generation: Feeling OK
About Living with Mom and Dad." Pew Research Center,
March 15, 2012. Retrieved April 2012 (http://www
.pewsocialtrends.org/2012/03/15/
the-boomerang-generation/?src=prc-headline).

Peck, Don. Pinched: How the Great Recession Has
Narrowed Our Futures and What We Can Do About It.
New York, NY: Crown Publishers, 2011.

Puzzanghera, Jim. "Financial Reform Gets Senate OK." Los
Angeles Times, June 16, 2010. Retrieved April 2012
(http://www.garp.org/risk-news-and-resources/risk
-headlines/story.aspx?altTemplate=PrintYellowBrix
Story&newsId=15114).

Rauchway, Eric. The Great Depression and the New Deal: A
Very Short Introduction. New York, NY: Oxford University
Press, 2008.

Roubini, Nouriel. *Crisis Economics: A Crash Course in the Future of Finance.* New York, NY: Penguin Press, 2010.

Schwartz, Nelson D. "Bank of America Makes Deal on Housing." *New York Times*, March 8, 2012. Retrieved April 2012 (http://www.nytimes.com/2012/03/09/business/bank-of-america-makes-deal-on-housing.html).

Suskind, Ron. *Confidence Men: Wall Street, Washington, and the Education of a President.* New York, NY: HarperCollins, 2011.

Tedesco, Theresa. "The Great Solvent North." *New York Times*, February 27, 2009. Retrieved April 2012 (http://www.nytimes.com/2009/02/28/opinion/28tedesco.html).

U.S. Government Accountability Office. "The Effect of the 2007–2009 Recession on Older Adults." October 18, 2011. Retrieved April 2012 (http://www.gao.gov/products/GAO-12-172T).

von Wachter, Till. "Long-Term Unemployment: Causes, Consequences, and Solutions." Testimony before the Joint Economic Committee of U.S. Congress, April 29, 2010. Retrieved April 2012 (http://www.columbia.edu/~vw2112/testimony_JEC_vonWachter_29April2010.pdf).

Wial, Howard. "MetroMonitor: Tracking Economic Recession and Recovery in America's 100 Largest Metropolitan Areas." Brookings Institute, March 28, 2012. Retrieved April 2012 (http://www.brookings.edu/reports/2011/0622_metro_monitor.aspx).

About the Author

Jason Porterfield is a journalist and writer living in Chicago, Illinois. He graduated from Oberlin College, where he majored in English, history, and religion. He has written more than twenty books for Rosen Publishing, including *How a Depression Works.*

Photo Credits